In the Spotlight

Neil deGrasse Tyson

by Kaitlyn Duling

Bullfrog Books

Ideas for Parents and Teachers

Bullfrog Books let children practice reading informational text at the earliest reading levels. Repetition, familiar words, and photo labels support early readers.

Before Reading

- Discuss the cover photo. What does it tell them?
- Look at the picture glossary together. Read and discuss the words.

Read the Book

- "Walk" through the book and look at the photos. Let the child ask questions. Point out the photo labels.
- Read the book to the child, or have him or her read independently.

After Reading

- Prompt the child to think more. Ask: What did you know about Neil deGrasse Tyson before reading this book? What more would you like to learn about him after reading it?

Bullfrog Books are published by Jump!
5357 Penn Avenue South
Minneapolis, MN 55419
www.jumplibrary.com

Library of Congress Cataloging-in-Publication Data

Names: Duling, Kaitlyn, author.
Title: Neil deGrasse Tyson / by Kaitlyn Duling.
Description: Minneapolis, MN : Jump!, Inc., [2019]
Series: Bullfrog books. In the spotlight
"Bullfrog Books are published by Jump!"
Audience: Ages 5–8. | Audience: K to grade 3.
Identifiers: LCCN 2018020127 (print)
LCCN 2018023667 (ebook)
ISBN 9781641282093 (e-book)
ISBN 9781641282079 (hardcover : alk. paper)
ISBN 9781641282086 (pbk.)
Subjects: LCSH: Tyson, Neil deGrasse—Juvenile literature. | Astrophysicists—United States Biography—Juvenile literature. | Astronautics United States—History—Juvenile literature.
Classification: LCC QB460.72.T97 (ebook)
LCC QB460.72.T97 D85 2018 (print)
DDC 523.01092 [B]—dc23
LC record available at https://lccn.loc.gov/2018020127

Editors: Susanne Bushman & Kristine Spanier
Designer: Molly Ballanger

Photo Credits: Robin Marchant/Getty, cover; Jason LaVeris/Getty, 1; Mike Coppola/Getty, 3; Imeh Akpanudosen/Getty, 4, 22tl; FOX/Getty, 5, 8–9, 10–11; adventtr/iStock, 6–7, 23br; Ben Molyneux/Alamy, 12, 22tr; Frederick M. Brown/Getty, 13; Bill Ingalls/NASA, 14–15; Sean Zanni/Getty, 16; Taylor Hill/Getty, 17; Vladimir Weinstein/BFA/REX/Shutterstock, 18–19; John Badman/AP Images, 20–21; DenisTangneyJr/iStock, 22tl; Mickey Adair/Getty, 22b; Tony Craddock/Shutterstock, 23tr; avid_creative/iStock, 23bl; WENN/Alamy, 24.

Printed in the United States of America at Corporate Graphics in North Mankato, Minnesota.

Table of Contents

Neil

This is Neil deGrasse Tyson.

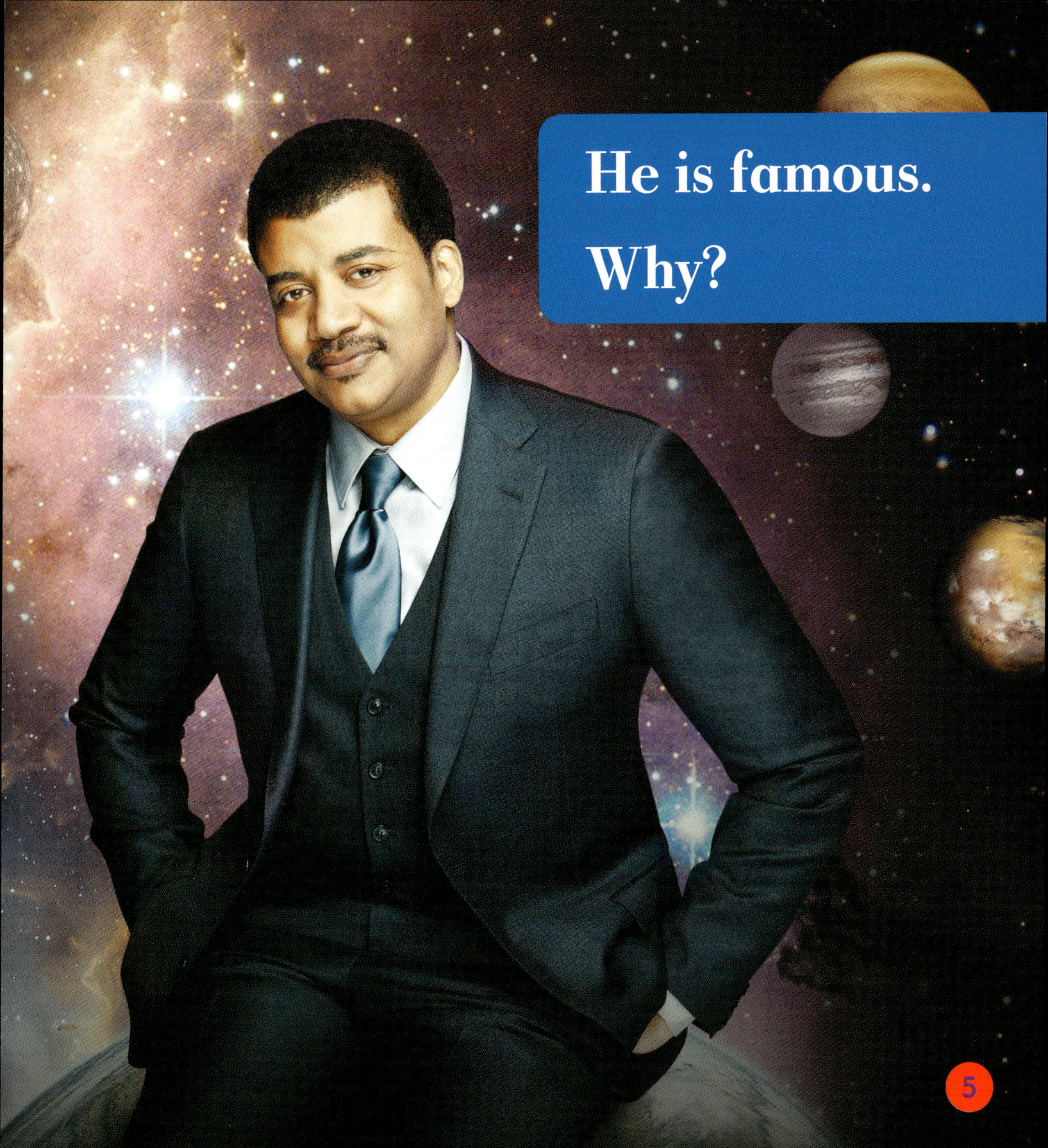

He is famous.

Why?

He studies stars.

What else?

Planets.

Our solar system.

Cool!

planet

Neil is on TV.

His show is called *Cosmos*.

He teaches.

He makes science easy to understand.

Wow!

book

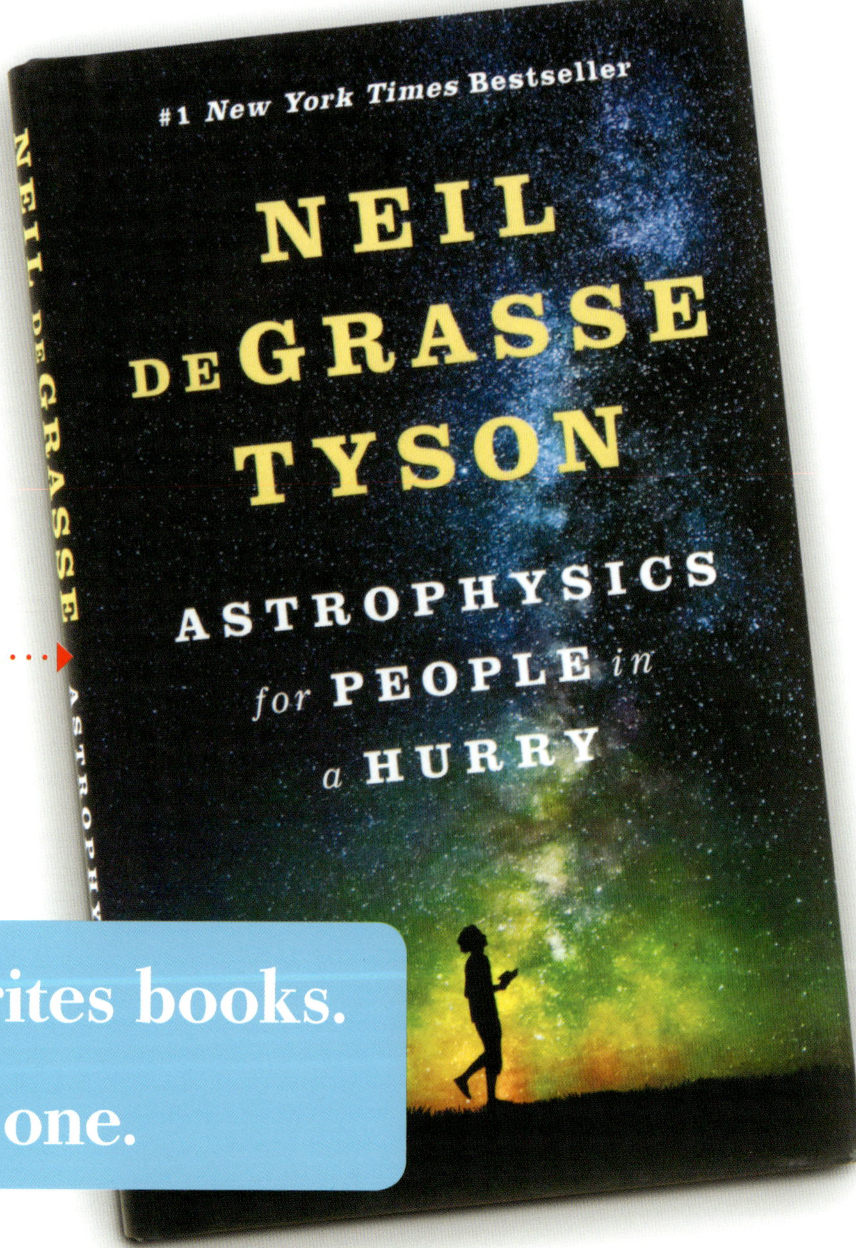

Neil writes books.

This is one.

He helps us learn.

APOLLO
4
YEARS
NASA
APOLLO
4
YEARS

He talks to leaders.

He gives them new ideas.

He worked with NASA!

Neil can be serious.

He can be funny, too.

Neil believes in you.

You can be a scientist, too!

He learns and teaches.

Thank you, Neil!

telescope

Key Events

October 5, 1958:
Neil deGrasse Tyson is born in the Bronx in New York City.

December 20, 1975:
Neil meets Carl Sagan, a famous astronomer who inspired Neil to study science and space.

May 3, 2007:
Time magazine names Neil one of the 100 most influential people in the world.

January 26, 2009:
Neil releases *The Pluto Files*, a book that explains why Pluto is a dwarf planet.

November 7, 2012:
Neil appears in *Action Comics*, a comic about Superman.

May 2, 2017:
Neil releases *Astrophysics for People in a Hurry*. This book spends more than a year on the New York Times Best Sellers List.

Picture Glossary

famous
Very well-known to many people.

NASA
The agency responsible for the space program and space research.

scientists
People who study science and the physical world or universe.

solar system
The sun and other planets that revolve around it.

Index

To Learn More

Finding more information is as easy as 1, 2, 3.

1. Go to www.factsurfer.com
2. Enter "NeildeGrasseTyson" into the search box.
3. Click the "Surf" button to see a list of websites.